The Joy of the Gospel

A six-session study course
in sharing faith

D1375215

Paula Gooder

CHURCH HOUSE
PUBLISHING

Church House Publishing
Church House
Great Smith Street
London SW1P 3AZ

First published 2015
Second impression 2016

Typeset by ForDesign

Printed and bound by CPI (UK) Ltd, Croydon

Contents

Preface

It was clear from the initial response to *The Joy of the Gospel* at the English Anglican–Roman Catholic Committee that there was a very significant opportunity here for deepening relationships between Catholics and Anglicans. Although Pope Francis is speaking in this apostolic exhortation in a particular way to his own Church, his profound and inspiring exposition of how a transformative commitment to sharing the gospel springs from our common baptism speaks to all believers. While some of the detail of the text focuses on specific issues in the Roman Catholic Church, much of it is transferable and all churches face parallel challenges in seeking to communicate the joy of the gospel in the world today.

We were therefore delighted when Paula Gooder (a member of the Anglican–Roman Catholic International Commission, ARCIC III) took up an invitation from the Committee to produce a study course that would help Anglicans and Christians of other traditions, as well as Catholics, engage with the rich themes of this text. While a variety of resources quickly became available to support individuals and groups studying *The Joy of the Gospel*, our impression was that these tended to be aimed at Catholics only. Paula's work will open up Pope Francis' words for a whole range of Christians, either to study the document in groups within their own churches or bringing people together from different churches. We hope in particular that this resource will enable Anglicans and Roman Catholics to meet together and reflect on how responding to Pope Francis' exhortation might encourage them to work together in sharing the gospel with their local communities.

Since its inception in 1970, the English Anglican–Roman Catholic Committee, part of a network of such groups around the world, has regularly given time to reading international documents with a bearing on relations between our churches. *The Joy of the Gospel* seeks to foster a renewed commitment to the common task of evangelization at every level of church life that could transform those relations profoundly. We are deeply grateful to Paula for providing a resource that will help to realize that potential, and we commend it warmly to our churches.

The Most Revd Bernard Longley
Archbishop of Birmingham

The Rt Revd Tim Thornton
Bishop of Truro

Co-chairs of the English Anglican–Roman Catholic Committee

Introduction

Documents from the Vatican are not often described as exciting. They are regularly important, authoritative, thought provoking, even challenging but very rarely exciting. Since the *The Joy of the Gospel* (*Evangelii Gaudium*) was published in 2013 I have lost track of the number of times that people have said to me 'You really must read this, it is so uplifting/inspiring/exciting'. They were right. *The Joy of the Gospel* is a rare document: it manages to capture something profound about the joy that comes from proclaiming the gospel and to put it into words in such a way that it is hard not to be infected by this enthusiastic vision for what it means for each one of us as Christians.

The document is an Apostolic Exhortation written to challenge and inspire people rather than to set doctrine. It was the first teaching document that Pope Francis wrote alone (a previous encyclical *Lumen Fidei* or the *Light of Faith* he wrote with Pope Emeritus Benedict XVI). Like most Apostolic Exhortations *The Joy of the Gospel* emerged out of a Synod of Bishops. The Synod of Bishops acts as an advisory body to the pope and has both Ordinary General Assemblies (those which meet regularly) and Extraordinary General Assemblies (those which meet occasionally).

The Synod of Bishops was first established at the end of the Second Vatican Council in 1965 by Pope Paul VI to support and advise the pope in his work. Strikingly the very first Apostolic Exhortation was published in 1975 by Pope Paul VI following a Synod of Bishops in 1974 on evangelization and was called *Evangelii Nuntiandi* (*Evangelization in the Modern World*); portions of this document were written by a Polish bishop Karol Wojtyla, who later became Pope John Paul II. If you read the full text of *The Joy of the Gospel* you will be able to see in the footnotes how influential the thinking of these two former popes has been on the mind of Pope Francis.

Just like previous Apostolic Exhortations, *The Joy of the Gospel* emerged out of an Ordinary General Assembly. In October 2012 the Synod of Bishops met to discuss the subject of 'The New Evangelization for the Transmission of the Christian Faith'. *The Joy of the Gospel*, however, though working from the synodal draft documents, is not entirely dependent on them. The Synod certainly influenced the pope's thinking but here he chose to 'take everything from the synod but put it in a wider framework'. This document then reflects the thinking expressed at the Synod but also presents the pope's own thinking on the subject.

Given the importance of the Synod of Bishops on the 'New Evangelization' for the writing of *The Joy of the Gospel*, following this introduction there is a brief reflection on the Synod of Bishops by the Rt Revd Steven Croft who was present at the Synod, representing the Church of England.

Some readers of this course will already have read *The Joy of the Gospel*, others will not. Some will take the opportunity of doing this course to read it in its entirety; others will only have the time to read limited parts of it. Whatever category you fall into, this course seeks to introduce you to some of the key ideas in the document and to provide a framework within which groups can study its ideas together. Some of the groups which use this course will be ecumenical; others will be drawn from just one denomination.

What is important is that we do study it and allow ourselves to be excited – or re-excited – by the joy that we ourselves encounter in the good news of Jesus and the joy we can feel when we begin to share that good news with others. It is this joy that radiates from Pope Francis himself and offers us a beacon of what we might become if only we can take this message seriously.

The sessions

Before each session of this course you will find a brief summary of the contents of the chapter it draws on, along with some more extended passages from that chapter. These are not intended to be read in your group but are for those people who have the time to spend ten to twenty minutes before the session familiarizing themselves with some of the key passages of *The Joy of the Gospel*. You do not need to have read these to be able to take part in the course. If you are unfamiliar with Catholic terminology, you might find it helpful to have the brief glossary at the end of this course (p. 52) to hand as you read.

Each session of this course will begin in the study of and reflection on Scripture and end with a short time of prayer. The main part of each session is focused around two themes drawn from each of the chapters (including the Introduction) of *The Joy of the Gospel*. It must be said that the document is so rich and contains such profound comments that it was often hard to choose only two themes, but time constraints in a group study mean that it is impossible to explore more than two per session. The course will, inevitably, omit some elements of the document – if you have read it yourself and feel the lack of some key themes do feel free to introduce them into your discussion.

The study of Scripture

The Joy of the Gospel recommends a way of reading the Bible – a spiritual reading – which is often called *lectio divina*. It describes it as a 'particular way of listening to what the Lord wishes to tell us in his word and of letting ourselves be transformed by the Spirit' (152). At the same time Pope Francis reminds us that this kind of spiritual reading is as well as, not instead of, careful study of what the Bible says. He says that it should begin with a study of the central message of the text before going on to discern how that message speaks to our own lives. In the spirit of this kind of reading, the brief Bible studies at the start of each session will be accompanied by a few notes which will help readers get to grips with what the passage is saying before allowing time to listen carefully to what the Spirit is saying to you in it.

Summaries and questions

Each section of the session begins with a brief summary of a key point made in *The Joy of the Gospel*. You can either read this out loud or spend a few moments reading it in silence before you begin your discussion. Please feel free to discuss as many or as few of the questions as is best for your group, or indeed to use the summary as a starting-off point for your discussion.

Quotations

Throughout the sessions you will find short quotations from *The Joy of the Gospel*; if any of them catch your eye do take the time to talk about them. Throughout this course the numbers at the start of paragraphs (for example 19. Evangelization takes place ...), or in brackets, for example (152) refer to the paragraph numbers in *The Joy of the Gospel* document itself.

Closing worship

It will be important to finish your group time with prayer. You may like to have a time of open prayer where you share together your needs and concerns and pray for each other as you go onward into the week. Alternatively you may prefer to use the responses provided at the end of each session, or you might like to do both. Each session ends with the Lord's Prayer and the Grace.

Paula Gooder, July 2015

Passing on our faith

Listening

In October 2012, around 400 bishops, archbishops and cardinals from all over the world gathered for the Synod of Bishops in Rome. They were joined by eighty or so lay advisers and a small number of ecumenical 'fraternal delegates'. I was invited as the Anglican fraternal delegate.

A Synod of Bishops has only one subject on the agenda. This Synod was on 'The New Evangelization for the Transmission of the Christian Faith' – how we pass on the faith both within the Church and beyond it.

The first task was to listen carefully to what is happening across the world. We spent twelve days simply attending to five-minute prepared speeches (or interventions). Twelve of these were delivered every hour for five hours each day. Every regional bishops' meeting from every part of the world had prepared one of these interventions, responding to the working document of the Synod which set out the major themes of our conversation.

The listening was hard work. In a single hour we were told stories of the struggles of the Church to communicate the faith in Cambodia, rebuilding after genocide; in Canada, following the child sexual abuse scandals; in Hong Kong, following a renewal of catechesis; in Germany, in response to rapid secularization.

I went to the Synod expecting to hear two different narratives: a story of growth from the developing world and a story of struggle and decline from the Church across Europe and North America. Instead, it seemed to me that the Church all over the world is having the same conversation. That includes the Anglican Communion and the Church of England. At the heart of that conversation is the understanding that evangelism is very difficult and challenging at the present time. The world increasingly shares a global, secularizing, consumerist culture, particularly in its urban areas. It is challenging to communicate the Christian faith within this culture. Most of the conversations we have as a Church about resources and ministry flow from this simple truth.

Wrestling

This period of intense and challenging listening was followed by a period of reflection. The Synod divided into smaller groups which wrestled together with what they had heard and began to determine what advice they might offer to the pope. A working group drawn from across the Synod reflected on these themes and drew up two draft documents: a list of recommendations and resolutions, and an inspirational message to the Church which captured the main themes of the Synod. These were published on the final day. In this way, the experience of laity, priests and bishops on every continent is heard and distilled and finds its way into the response of the Church to what is undoubtedly an immensely challenging situation.

Renewing

Just a few months after the Synod of Bishops, Pope Benedict XVI who called the Synod, took the courageous decision to stand down. Pope Francis was elected by many of the cardinals who had listened and prayed in response to all that had been shared about the Church during those three weeks in Rome.

This background of listening to and living these difficult experiences is essential for understanding *The Joy of the Gospel*. As you prepare to explore its themes with others, it will be important to listen honestly to the difficulties the group experience in passing on the Christian faith in this generation to our children, to our friends and our neighbours.

The process of reflection undoubtedly moved on between the Synod and the Apostolic Exhortation. Some of this movement is undoubtedly because of the personal contribution of Pope Francis. Some pick up themes which are emerging in the final documents. But there are lessons here for the whole Church.

The first is undoubtedly the need to return again to the gospel, to the face of Christ, to appreciating again the profound truth of the gospel, to the reconversion of our own hearts and minds. It was moving to hear senior cardinals in the Synod cry out that it is we who need to be converted once again. This is, surely, the primary place for the Church to begin in the midst of a world which is finding it hard to hear the message we bring.

The second is the profound emphasis on joy which runs through the whole document and is present in the title. The joy which emerges flows from Christ and from Christ alone. It is the wellspring of hope and an authentic response to reading the Gospels afresh and beginning again from Christ.

The third is a renewed sense of what it means to be the Church and seeing the Church as a company of missionary disciples. The words 'mission' and 'disciple' were only rarely used in the presentations to the Synod of Bishops but they emerged during the group discussions as immensely helpful in describing what the Church needs to be and become in this present season.

The fourth is a restored confidence in the message we proclaim. This in turn leads to an encouragement both to retain confidence in the traditional means of evangelism and to be creative and bold in seeking new ways to communicate faith.

These four themes are vital to Christians of every church as we ponder the call to make disciples in our own generation. We, too, need to return to the gospel, to recover joy, to see the Church again as a company of missionary disciples and to proclaim the faith with compassion, with confidence and with creativity to a new generation.

Rt Revd Steven Croft
Bishop of Sheffield

The Joy of the Gospel

Summary of the Introduction, paragraphs 1–18

An encounter with Jesus brings deep and lasting joy. We live in a world that is so pervaded by consumerism that it breeds desolation, anguish and a feverish pursuit of frivolous pleasures. This is not God's will for us. Instead Christians are invited once again to a renewed personal encounter with Jesus Christ. The message of the Bible is that the joy of salvation would abound in messianic times. Running through the New Testament we find the strand of rejoicing: people are commanded to rejoice and they do rejoice time and time again. Joy finds a different expression in our lives at different times, especially during the particularly difficult times of life, but we are called to be Christians whose lives are as much influenced by Easter as by Lent.

When we encounter God's love how can we fail to share that love with others? We need not only to recover but to deepen our enthusiasm so that our lives glow with the fervour that comes from the joy of Christ. Mission is not, however, a heroic, individual undertaking. When we share the good news of the gospel we join in with the work of Jesus who is the first and the greatest evangelizer and he leads us in this by the power of his Spirit.

This exhortation arose out of the XIII Ordinary General Assembly of the Synod of Bishops (7–28 October 2012) which gathered to discuss 'The New Evangelization for the Transmission of the Christian Faith' and which reaffirmed three key themes: the importance of ordinary pastoral ministry; the need for the baptized whose lives do not reflect the demands of baptism to experience, once more, the joy of faith; and the centrality of proclaiming the gospel to those who do not know Christ. This exhortation, written by Pope Francis, reaps the rich fruits of the Synod's work.

Key extracts from the Introduction

(Numbers at the start of each paragraph refer to the paragraph numbers in the document)

1. The joy of the gospel fills the hearts and lives of all who encounter Jesus. Those who accept his offer of salvation are set free from sin, sorrow, inner emptiness and loneliness. With Christ joy is constantly born anew. In this Exhortation I wish to encourage the Christian faithful to embark upon a new chapter of evangelization marked by this joy, while pointing out new paths for the Church's journey in years to come. A joy ever new, a joy which is shared

2. The great danger in today's world, pervaded as it is by consumerism, is the desolation and anguish born of a complacent yet covetous heart, the feverish pursuit of frivolous pleasures, and a blunted conscience. Whenever our interior life becomes caught up in its own interests and concerns, there is no longer room for others, no place for the poor. God's voice is no longer heard, the quiet joy of his love is no longer felt, and the desire to do good fades. This is a very real danger for believers too. Many fall prey to it, and end up resentful, angry and listless. That is no way to live a dignified and fulfilled life; it is not God's will for us, nor is it the life in the Spirit which has its source in the heart of the risen Christ.

3. I invite all Christians, everywhere, at this very moment, to a renewed personal encounter with Jesus Christ, or at least an openness to letting him encounter them; I ask all of you to do this unfailingly each day. No one should think that this invitation is not meant for him or her, since 'no one is excluded from the joy brought by the Lord'.

6. There are Christians whose lives seem like Lent without Easter. I realize of course that joy is not expressed the same way at all times in life, especially at moments of great difficulty. Joy adapts and changes, but it always endures, even as a flicker of light born of our personal certainty that, when everything is said and done, we are infinitely loved. I understand the grief of people who have to endure great suffering, yet slowly but surely we all have to let the joy of faith slowly revive as a quiet yet firm trust, even amid the greatest distress: 'My soul is bereft of peace; I have forgotten what happiness is ... But this I call to mind, and therefore I have hope: the

steadfast love of the Lord never ceases, his mercies never come to an end; they are new every morning. Great is your faithfulness … It is good that one should wait quietly for the salvation of the Lord' (Lam 3.17, 21–23, 26).

9. Goodness always tends to spread. Every authentic experience of truth and goodness seeks by its very nature to grow within us, and any person who has experienced a profound liberation becomes more sensitive to the needs of others. As it expands, goodness takes root and develops. If we wish to lead a dignified and fulfilling life, we have to reach out to others and seek their good. In this regard, several sayings of Saint Paul will not surprise us: 'The love of Christ urges us on' (2 Cor. 5.14); 'Woe to me if I do not proclaim the gospel' (1 Cor. 9.16).

Joy and the Gospel

Our faith in Jesus brings joy,
a joy that we must share

Reflection on Scripture together
Philippians 4.4–8

⁴Rejoice in the Lord always; again I will say, Rejoice. ⁵Let your gentleness be known to everyone. The Lord is near. ⁶Do not worry about anything, but in everything by prayer and supplication with thanksgiving let your requests be made known to God. ⁷And the peace of God, which surpasses all understanding, will guard your hearts and your minds in Christ Jesus.

⁸ Finally, beloved, whatever is true, whatever is honourable, whatever is just, whatever is pure, whatever is pleasing, whatever is commendable, if there is any excellence and if there is anything worthy of praise, think about these things.

Explanatory note

We learn in Philippians 1.7, 13 and 17 that Paul was in prison when he wrote this letter. The Philippians knew this and sent Epaphroditus with some help for Paul. Epaphroditus nearly died in the attempt (Philippians 2.25–27 and 4.18). This letter was written at a very hard time in Paul's life and yet the theme of joy is woven all the way through it.

The word translated 'Rejoice' here can also mean 'Greeting' (it is what Gabriel said to Mary in Luke 1.28). Its repetition here – and indeed the sense of the sentence – suggests that Paul is directing the Philippians to be people who not only greet God but find their joy in him.

- Ask someone to read the passage through; keep a few moments' silence.

- Read the explanatory note above and spend a few minutes discussing any points that you notice.

- Then read the passage again (asking someone else to read it this time).

- Invite everyone to say a word or phrase which strikes them from the passage.

- Read the passage a third time; share together what this word or phrase means to you in your life and what questions it raises.

Returning to the joy of the gospel (based on 1–8)

The joy of the gospel fills the hearts and lives of all who encounter Jesus … With Christ joy is constantly born anew. (1)

I invite all Christians, everywhere, at this very moment, to a renewed personal encounter with Jesus Christ, or at least an openness to letting him encounter them: I ask all of you to do this unfailingly each day. (3)

Joy adapts and changes, but it always endures, even as a flicker of light born of our personal certainty that, when everything is said and done, we are infinitely loved … I understand the grief of people who have to endure great suffering, yet slowly but surely we all have to let the joy of faith slowly revive as a quiet yet firm trust, even amid the greatest distress. (6)

The experience of Christian faith is an experience of deep and lasting joy. This joy finds its roots in the knowledge that God loves us and will never stop. Of course joy cannot be expressed the same way at all times in life, especially when you are going through a difficult time, but the joy that comes from God's love for us never fails. The message of joy runs all the way through the Bible from the Prophets to the Gospels and Paul. This message requires us to recognize God's presence with us and to allow him to bring us beyond ourselves so that we can become the fullest truth of who God wants us to be.

Discuss

Spend some time in the group sharing examples of occasions when you have felt this kind of joy.

This joy comes from a renewed personal encounter with Jesus or from an openness to allow him to encounter us. What would we need to do in our everyday lives to ensure that we are open to encounters with Jesus and to the joy that this brings?

How is it possible for the joy of faith to revive you after suffering? What would that mean in practice? If you have had experience of this, share it with the group.

The joy of evangelizing
(based on 9–18)

Goodness always tends to spread … As it expands, goodness takes root and develops. If we wish to lead a dignified and fulfilling life, we have to reach out to others and seek their good. (9)

Whenever we make the effort to return to the source and to recover the original freshness of the Gospel, new avenues arise, new paths of creativity open up, with different forms of expression, more eloquent signs and words with new meaning for today's world. Every form of authentic evangelization is always 'new'. (11)

Jesus is 'the first and greatest evangelizer'. (12)

Joy is not true joy if we keep it to ourselves. The joy of the good news of Jesus Christ demands to be shared. If it is not shared the joy weakens and withers away. Sharing the good news of what God has done for us in Jesus Christ will renew our faith and enable us to be amazed again at the 'depth of the riches and wisdom and knowledge of God' (Romans 11.33). When we share this good news authentically, we will discover new riches and wisdom because true evangelism is always new.

Discuss

Does the thought of sharing your faith fill you with joy? With dread? With enthusiasm? With fear? Share a little of how you feel about sharing your faith and what you might need for the thought to fill you with joy.

Can you think of any examples in which goodness has spread and begun to make a difference?

What do you think the 'original freshness of the Gospel' is?

Closing worship

Light a candle – have a few moments of silence.

In the silence think about

- anything that has particularly challenged you in this session
- if there is anything you want to do differently from now on.

Spend a few minutes sharing your thoughts together, before either moving into a time of prayer or praying the final responses and prayers together.

Loving God, you show us the path to life
In your presence is fullness of joy

Your steadfast love endures for ever
In your presence is fullness of joy

You are the source of all good news
In your presence is fullness of joy

How beautiful are the feet of the messengers who bring good news
In your presence is fullness of joy

Amen

(taken from Psalm 16.11; Isaiah 52.7)

As our Saviour taught us, so we pray: **Our Father**

And

**may the grace of our Lord Jesus Christ,
and the love of God,
and the fellowship of the Holy Spirit
be with us all
evermore.**

Amen.

The Church's Missionary Transformation

Summary of Chapter 1, paragraphs 19–49

We proclaim the gospel in obedience to Jesus' command in Matthew 28.19–20 to make disciples of all nations. All through the Bible God challenges those who believe in him to 'Go forth' from their comfort zones and to reach those on the outskirts who are in need of the light of the good news. This proclamation plants the seeds of the gospel which, once sown, is unpredictable in its power and grows and grows. The Church is called to be a community of missionary disciples, rooted in the knowledge of the love of God, which then shows that love to all those around. This community is supportive and patient as it waits for the seed to grow and celebrates every sign of the fruitfulness of the Gospel.

We need to be in a permanent state of mission and prepared to transform the structures of our Church so that our work can be as inclusive as possible. All aspects of Church life are called to missionary conversion so that they are ready for the work of reaching outwards. This will inevitably affect the way in which we communicate the message, which will become more simple and convincing while losing none of its depth. In order to achieve this the Church needs to grow in interpretation of the revealed word of God and in an understanding of truth. A Church that goes forth is a Church whose doors are always open. It is tempting to rush outwards, aimlessly into the world, but it is often better to slow down, to see and listen to what people are saying and to keep our doors open so that when people do return they are welcomed warmly. When the Church does go out, it should go first to the poor and the sick and be prepared to be bruised, hurting and dirty because it has been out on the streets among the poor.

Key extracts from Chapter 1

(Numbers at the start of each paragraph refer to the paragraph numbers in the document)

19. Evangelization takes place in obedience to the missionary mandate of Jesus: 'Go therefore and make disciples of all nations, baptizing them in the name of the Father and of the Son and of the Holy Spirit, teaching them to observe all that I have commanded you' (Mt 28.19–20). In these verses we see how the risen Christ sent his followers to preach the Gospel in every time and place, so that faith in him might spread to every corner of the earth.

22. God's word is unpredictable in its power. The Gospel speaks of a seed which, once sown, grows by itself, even as the farmer sleeps (Mk 4.26–29). The Church has to accept this unruly freedom of the word, which accomplishes what it wills in ways that surpass our calculations and ways of thinking.

24. The Church which 'goes forth' is a community of missionary disciples who take the first step, who are involved and supportive, who bear fruit and rejoice … An evangelizing community gets involved by word and deed in people's daily lives; it bridges distances, it is willing to abase itself if necessary, and it embraces human life, touching the suffering flesh of Christ in others. Evangelizers thus take on the 'smell of the sheep' and the sheep are willing to hear their voice. An evangelizing community is also supportive, standing by people at every step of the way, no matter how difficult or lengthy this may prove to be. It is familiar with patient expectation and apostolic endurance. Evangelization consists mostly of patience and disregard for constraints of time.

27. I dream of a 'missionary option', that is, a missionary impulse capable of transforming everything, so that the Church's customs, ways of doing things, times and schedules, language and structures can be suitably channelled for the evangelization of today's world rather than for her self-preservation. The renewal of structures demanded by pastoral conversion can only be understood in this light: as part of an effort to make them more mission-oriented, to make ordinary pastoral activity on every level more inclusive and open, to inspire in pastoral

workers a constant desire to go forth and in this way to elicit a positive response from all those whom Jesus summons to friendship with himself.

49. Let us go forth, then, let us go forth to offer everyone the life of Jesus Christ. Here I repeat for the entire Church what I have often said to the priests and laity of Buenos Aires: I prefer a Church which is bruised, hurting and dirty because it has been out on the streets, rather than a Church which is unhealthy from being confined and from clinging to its own security. I do not want a Church concerned with being at the centre and which then ends by being caught up in a web of obsessions and procedures. If something should rightly disturb us and trouble our consciences, it is the fact that so many of our brothers and sisters are living without the strength, light and consolation born of friendship with Jesus Christ, without a community of faith to support them, without meaning and a goal in life. More than by fear of going astray, my hope is that we will be moved by the fear of remaining shut up within structures which give us a false sense of security, within rules which make us harsh judges, within habits which make us feel safe, while at our door people are starving and Jesus does not tire of saying to us: 'Give them something to eat' (Mk 6.37).

2

Going Forth

The importance of being an outward-facing Church, always ready to be sent forth by God

Reflection on Scripture together
Matthew 28.16–20

[16]Now the eleven disciples went to Galilee, to the mountain to which Jesus had directed them. [17]When they saw him, they worshipped him; but some doubted. [18]And Jesus came and said to them, 'All authority in heaven and on earth has been given to me. [19]Go therefore and make disciples of all nations, baptizing them in the name of the Father and of the Son and of the Holy Spirit, [20]and teaching them to obey everything that I have commanded you. And remember, I am with you always, to the end of the age.'

Explanatory note

In Matthew's Gospel nearly all references to 'disciples' are to the twelve whom he called to follow him. That changes here where Jesus sends these disciples out to make disciples of all nations. Jesus' final command to his disciples is to 'go forth'.

One of the problems of the word 'go' is that it implies that Jesus sends them and then stays behind. The word translated 'go' here actually means 'to travel'. Jesus then says 'and remember I am with you always'. In other words, his command is to 'come' with him on the adventure of making new disciples.

● Ask someone to read the passage through; keep a few moments' silence.

- Read the explanatory note above and spend a few minutes discussing any points that you notice.

- Then read the passage again (asking someone else to read it this time).

- Invite everyone to say a word or phrase which strikes them from the passage.

- Read the passage a third time; share together what this word or phrase means to you in your life and what questions it raises.

A Church which goes forth
(based on 19–33)

Q

Each Christian and every community must discern the path that the Lord points out, but all of us are asked to obey his call to go forth from our own comfort zone in order to reach all the 'peripheries' in need of the light of the gospel. (20)

There are ecclesial structures which can hamper efforts at evangelization, yet even good structures are only helpful when there is a life constantly driving, sustaining and assessing them. (26)

[The Parish] is a sanctuary where the thirsty come to drink in the midst of their journey, and a centre of constant missionary outreach. (28)

Pastoral ministry in a missionary key seeks to abandon the complacent attitude that says: 'We have always done it this way'. (33)

The Church is called to be a community of missionary disciples sent outwards by Christ to show his love in the world. This task requires us to get involved in people's lives, to support them, to stand with them patiently no matter how long this might take. An evangelizing community is concerned with fruitfulness but does not grow impatient with the weeds as it waits for seeds to bear fruit. Evangelizing communities need to be communities open to conversion themselves, constantly prepared to change their structures so that they are permeated with life, so that they can be found wherever the need for the light and life of the risen Christ is greatest.

Discuss

What do you already do – either as an individual or as a church community – to go beyond your comfort zone and show Christ's love to the world? Is there anything you need to do more?

In your view what one church structure most hampers the sharing of the gospel where you live? What would you do to change it?

If we organized our churches/parishes around the principle of being a source of refreshment to the thirsty and a 'constant centre of missionary outreach', what kinds of activities might we do? And what might we stop doing?

A house with the doors always open
(based on 34–49)

Q

When we adopt a pastoral goal and a missionary style which would actually reach everyone without exception or exclusion, the message has to concentrate on the essentials, on what is most beautiful, most grand, most appealing and at the same time most necessary. (35)

The Church is called to be the house of the Father, with doors always wide open ... Frequently, we act as arbiters of grace rather than its facilitators. (47)

I prefer a Church which is bruised, hurting and dirty because it has been out on the streets, rather than a Church which is unhealthy from being confined and from clinging to its own security. (49)

This will also affect how we communicate the message of the gospel, a communication which should be clear and simple but at the same time beautiful, grand and appealing. In making what we say clear we should not lose any of the gospel's depth and truth. In order to do this the Church needs to grow in her understanding of truth, with the help of exegetes, theologians and other academic disciplines. Although some people long for monolithic doctrine that leaves no room for nuance, the reality is that variety brings out and develops different facets of the inexhaustible riches of the gospel. God calls the Church to have its doors wide open, both literally and figuratively so that all can come in and find a home. He also sends the Church forth. First and foremost he sends us to the poor and the sick with the command to give them something to eat.

Discuss

How might we proclaim the message of the gospel simply in the twenty-first century in such a way as also maintains its beauty, depth and truth? Can you remember when you last encountered this kind of proclamation?

If we were to become communities with our doors wide open, what would we need to be and do to make this possible?

How do you relate to the idea of the Church being 'bruised, hurting and dirty' because it has been on the streets?

Closing worship

Light a candle – have a few moments of silence.

In the silence think about

● anything that has particularly challenged you in this session

● if there is anything you want to do differently from now on.

Spend a few minutes sharing your thoughts together, before either moving into a time of prayer or praying the final responses and prayers together.

Lord Jesus Christ, we hear your call to go forth into the world
Knowing you will be with us to the end of the age

We go to seek the lost, the poor and the sick
Knowing you will be with us to the end of the age

We fling wide the doors of our churches and our hearts
Knowing you will be with us to the end of the age

We offer rest to the weary and refreshment to the thirsty
Knowing you will be with us to the end of the age

Amen

(taken from Matthew 28.16–21)

As our Saviour taught us, so we pray: **Our Father**

And

**may the grace of our Lord Jesus Christ,
and the love of God,
and the fellowship of the Holy Spirit
be with us all
evermore.**

Amen.

Amid the Crisis of Communal Commitment

Summary of Chapter 2, paragraphs 50–109

The characteristics of the world in which we live are well rehearsed and diagnosed. Nevertheless it is important for all communities to watch carefully for the 'signs of the times' so that they can discern what is the fruit of the kingdom and what runs counter to God's plan. We need to say no to an economic system that excludes people; to the idolatry of money; to a financial system which rules over us rather than serves us; to an inequality of wealth that spawns violence. We need to confront a modern desire to give precedence to appearances rather than to what is real and to the argument that attempts to reduce faith to the private and personal. We also need to evangelize cultures so that they contain strands of faith and solidarity. Within cities there is a particular need to understand the culture of that place so that we can enter into a proper dialogue with it.

There are some particular temptations that face people involved in pastoral work. They need to resist the temptation to see their work as an appendage to their life, or their spiritual life as the following of a few exercises that will bring personal comfort and instead see it as something that encourages engagement with others. They need to resist selfishness and spiritual laziness, defeatism and pessimism and instead to find Jesus in the faces of others. They need to avoid spiritual worldliness, which hides behind piety and love for the Church, warring among each other and instead to embrace the law of love. They need to encourage the gifts of those who are currently not fully engaged in the ministry of the Church: lay people in general, women and young people. We face many challenges but they exist to be overcome!

Key extracts from Chapter 2

(Numbers at the start of each paragraph refer to the paragraph numbers in the document)

51. It is not the task of the Pope to offer a detailed and complete analysis of contemporary reality, but I do exhort all the communities to an 'ever watchful scrutiny of the signs of the times'. This is in fact a grave responsibility, since certain present realities, unless effectively dealt with, are capable of setting off processes of dehumanization which would then be hard to reverse. We need to distinguish clearly what might be a fruit of the kingdom from what runs counter to God's plan. This involves not only recognizing and discerning spirits, but also – and this is decisive – choosing movements of the spirit of good and rejecting those of the spirit of evil.

52. In our time humanity is experiencing a turning-point in its history, as we can see from the advances being made in so many fields. We can only praise the steps being taken to improve people's welfare in areas such as health care, education and communications. At the same time we have to remember that the majority of our contemporaries are barely living from day to day, with dire consequences. A number of diseases are spreading. The hearts of many people are gripped by fear and desperation, even in the so-called rich countries. The joy of living frequently fades, lack of respect for others and violence are on the rise, and inequality is increasingly evident. It is a struggle to live and, often, to live with precious little dignity. This epochal change has been set in motion by the enormous qualitative, quantitative, rapid and cumulative advances occurring in the sciences and in technology, and by their instant application in different areas of nature and of life. We are in an age of knowledge and information, which has led to new and often anonymous kinds of power.

53. Just as the commandment 'Thou shalt not kill' sets a clear limit in order to safeguard the value of human life, today we also have to say 'Thou shalt not' to an economy of exclusion and inequality. Such an economy kills. How can it be that it is not a news item when an elderly homeless person dies of exposure, but it is news when the stock market loses

two points? This is a case of exclusion. Can we continue to stand by when food is thrown away while people are starving? This is a case of inequality. Today everything comes under the laws of competition and the survival of the fittest, where the powerful feed upon the powerless. As a consequence, masses of people find themselves excluded and marginalized: without work, without possibilities, without any means of escape.

81.   At a time when we most need a missionary dynamism which will bring salt and light to the world, many lay people fear that they may be asked to undertake some apostolic work and they seek to avoid any responsibility that may take away from their free time. For example, it has become very difficult today to find trained parish catechists willing to persevere in this work for some years. Something similar is also happening with priests who are obsessed with protecting their free time. This is frequently due to the fact that people feel an overbearing need to guard their personal freedom, as though the task of evangelization was a dangerous poison rather than a joyful response to God's love which summons us to mission and makes us fulfilled and productive. Some resist giving themselves over completely to mission and thus end up in a state of paralysis and acedia.

83.   And so the biggest threat of all gradually takes shape: 'the gray pragmatism of the daily life of the Church, in which all appears to proceed normally, while in reality faith is wearing down and degenerating into small-mindedness'. A tomb psychology thus develops and slowly transforms Christians into mummies in a museum. Disillusioned with reality, with the Church and with themselves, they experience a constant temptation to cling to a faint melancholy, lacking in hope, which seizes the heart like 'the most precious of the devil's potions'. Called to radiate light and communicate life, in the end they are caught up in things that generate only darkness and inner weariness, and slowly consume all zeal for the apostolate. For all this, I repeat: Let us not allow ourselves to be robbed of the joy of evangelization!

3

Saying Yes and Saying No

The need to become a community which resists those things that deprive us of life and instead embraces the love of God

Reflection on Scripture together

1 Peter 2.9–12

[9]But you are a chosen race, a royal priesthood, a holy nation, God's own people, in order that you may proclaim the mighty acts of him who called you out of darkness into his marvellous light. [10]Once you were not a people, but now you are God's people; once you had not received mercy, but now you have received mercy. [11]Beloved, I urge you as aliens and exiles to abstain from the desires of the flesh that wage war against the soul. [12]Conduct yourselves honourably among the Gentiles, so that, though they malign you as evildoers, they may see your honourable deeds and glorify God when he comes to judge.

Explanatory note

The descriptions of God's people that 1 Peter chooses to use here are drawn from two passages in the Old Testament: Isaiah 43.20–21 and Exodus 19.6. The first, chosen race, and last, God's own people, come from Isaiah 43.20–21 (my chosen people; the people whom I formed for myself) and the middle two, royal priesthood and holy nation, come from Exodus 19.6 (priestly kingdom and holy nation). Thus there is a reference to the two great events of Israel's history: the Exodus and the return from Exile. Verse 10 also contains a reference to Hosea 1.6 and 9 (not my people and not pitied). They are people with a fine heritage.

The word translated 'honourably' in verse 12 translates the word *kalos* in Greek which has a range of meanings including fine, good, noble and magnificent. In other words, the people are being urged to live up to the heritage they have by living nobly.

- Ask someone to read the passage through; keep a few moments, silence.

- Read the explanatory note above and spend a few minutes discussing any points that you notice.

- Then read the passage again (asking someone else to read it this time).

- Invite everyone to say a word or phrase which strikes them from the passage.

- Read the passage a third time; share together what this word or phrase means to you in your life and what questions it raises.

Discerning what runs counter to God's plan (based on 50–75)

Q

We need to distinguish clearly what might be a fruit of the kingdom from what runs counter to God's plan. (51)

To sustain a lifestyle which excludes others, or to sustain enthusiasm for that selfish ideal, a globalization of indifference has developed. Almost without being aware of it, we end up being incapable of feeling compassion at the outcry of the poor, weeping for other people's pain, and feeling a need to help them, as though all this were someone else's responsibility and not our own. (54)

The process of secularization tends to reduce the faith and the Church to the sphere of the private and personal. (64)

The challenge for all Christians is to discern what in our culture bears the fruit of the kingdom and what runs against God's plan for the world. We need to become people who recognize, discern and choose movements of the spirit of good while rejecting those of the spirit of evil. In a world that has made so many advances while at the same time cultural diseases are spreading, diseases like fear, desperation, violence and inequality, we need to oppose anything that treats humanity as consumer goods to be used and then discarded. We need to oppose inequality and exclusion; the idolatry of money; a financial system that rules over us rather than serving us. We need to oppose a growing secularization that reduces faith and the Church to the private sphere.

Discuss

Do you agree with Pope Francis' diagnosis of our global world as driven by consumerism, greed, inequality and exclusion? If you were to characterize the 'signs of the times' what words would you use to describe the twenty-first-century world we live in?

What contributes to the 'globalization of indifference' and how do we resist it so that we *can* feel compassion at the outcry of the poor, weep for other people's pain, and feel a need to help them'?

Why do you think that secularization tries to reduce faith and the Church to the private and personal sphere? What role ought faith and the Church to have in the public square?

Particular challenges for those within the Church (based on 76–109)

> **Q**
>
> The spiritual life comes to be identified with a few religious exercises which can offer a certain comfort but which do not encourage encounter with others, engagement with the world or a passion for evangelization. (78)
>
> The problem is not always an excess of activity, but rather activity undertaken badly, without adequate motivation, without a spirituality which would permeate it and make it pleasurable. As a result, work becomes more tiring than necessary, even leading at times to illness. (82)
>
> One of the more serious temptations which stifles boldness and zeal is a defeatism which turns us into querulous and disillusioned pessimists, 'sourpusses'. (85)
>
> Challenges exist to be overcome! Let us be realists, but without losing our joy, our boldness and our hope-filled commitment. (109)

There are particular temptations that affect those who are committed to the Church. It is all too easy for them to see their pastoral work as an appendage to their normal life, rather than central to it. They can see their spiritual life as something they do for their own comfort and not something that sends them out to encounter others. There are many people within the Church who are doing a lot but their activity is not grounded in a spirituality which permeates it; as a result their work makes them more and more tired and sometimes even ill. One of the worst temptations of all is defeatism which turns us into 'querulous and disillusioned pessimists'. We need to resist these kinds of temptations and instead learn to embrace the love of God, to accept and esteem others as companions along the way and to find Jesus in their faces.

Discuss

What do you think are the major temptations that afflict those within the Church? Do you agree with the ones identified here? Would you want to add any more?

If you were to see your spiritual life not as something which brings personal comfort but which sends you out to encounter others, would there be anything that you need to do differently?

Pope Francis' description of 'a defeatism which turns us into querulous and disillusioned pessimists, "sourpusses"' is profoundly evocative. What is it, do you think, about church life that can so easily turn us into pessimists?

Closing worship

Light a candle – have a few moments of silence.

In the silence think about

● anything that has particularly challenged you in this session

● if there is anything you want to do differently from now on.

Spend a few minutes sharing your thoughts together, before either moving into a time of prayer or praying the final responses and prayers together.

God has chosen us to be his own people
So that we might proclaim his great and glorious deeds

He called us from darkness into light
So that we might proclaim his great and glorious deeds

He has made us a holy nation, a royal priesthood
So that we might proclaim his great and glorious deeds

He has made us his people and shown us mercy
So that we might proclaim his great and glorious deeds

Amen

(taken from 1 Peter 2.9–12)

As our Saviour taught us, so we pray: **Our Father**

And

may the grace of our Lord Jesus Christ,
and the love of God,
and the fellowship of the Holy Spirit
be with us all
evermore.

Amen.

The Proclamation of the Gospel

Summary of Chapter 3, paragraphs 110–175

God's salvation is for everyone and the entire people of God proclaim the gospel. It is the outpouring of his mercy. We cannot earn it. No one is saved by themself or because of their own effort. The Church must be a place where God's mercy is experienced and all feel welcome. The Church shows forth the 'beauty of her varied face' in the many different cultures of the world. It is important to recognize that no one culture has more ownership of the gospel than any other. Everyone who is baptized is called to be a missionary disciple, no matter how long they have been a Christian. We are all called to grow into greater maturity in our work as evangelizers but you do not have to wait to be mature before you begin. Evangelization can take many different forms. It can take place in the natural and spontaneous expression of popular piety. It can happen through conversation. It also needs to happen by communication with people at the top of their field in professional, scientific and academic circles.

One of the key features of good evangelization is knowing the message well ourselves. Within the Church this often can be achieved through good preaching. A homily in a eucharistic setting is much more than just teaching; it is the occasion when there is a dialogue between God and his people. It is much more than the communication of truth; it communicates the beauty of the images that Jesus first used. Preaching is so important that it takes great preparation: close attention needs to be given to the biblical text; the message needs to be given time to enter the heart of the preacher, and the needs of the people need to be heard and responded to. One way of paying close attention to what the Lord is saying is through praying the Scriptures – beginning with their literal sense but then going on to listen to what they have to say in daily life. As a result, evangelization will involve your own growth deeper into the love of God.

Key extracts from Chapter 3

(Numbers at the start of each paragraph refer to the paragraph numbers in the document)

112. The salvation which God offers us is the work of his mercy. No human efforts, however good they may be, can enable us to merit so great a gift. God, by his sheer grace, draws us to himself and makes us one with him. He sends his Spirit into our hearts to make us his children, transforming us and enabling us to respond to his love by our lives. The Church is sent by Jesus Christ as the sacrament of the salvation offered by God.

117. When properly understood, cultural diversity is not a threat to Church unity. The Holy Spirit, sent by the Father and the Son, transforms our hearts and enables us to enter into the perfect communion of the blessed Trinity, where all things find their unity. He builds up the communion and harmony of the people of God. The same Spirit is that harmony, just as he is the bond of love between the Father and the Son. It is he who brings forth a rich variety of gifts, while at the same time creating a unity which is never uniformity but a multifaceted and inviting harmony. Evangelization joyfully acknowledges these varied treasures which the Holy Spirit pours out upon the Church. We would not do justice to the logic of the incarnation if we thought of Christianity as monocultural and monotonous.

121. Of course, all of us are called to mature in our work as evangelizers. We want to have better training, a deepening love and a clearer witness to the gospel. In this sense, we ought to let others be constantly evangelizing us. But this does not mean that we should postpone the evangelizing mission; rather, each of us should find ways

to communicate Jesus wherever we are. All of us are called to offer others an explicit witness to the saving love of the Lord, who despite our imperfections offers us his closeness, his word and his strength, and gives meaning to our lives.

144. To speak from the heart means that our hearts must not just be on fire, but also enlightened by the fullness of revelation and by the path travelled by God's word in the heart of the Church and our faithful people throughout history. This Christian identity, as the baptismal embrace which the Father gave us when we were little ones, makes us desire, as prodigal children – and favourite children in Mary – yet another embrace, that of the merciful Father who awaits us in glory. Helping our people to feel that they live in the midst of these two embraces is the difficult but beautiful task of one who preaches the gospel.

152. There is one particular way of listening to what the Lord wishes to tell us in his word and of letting ourselves be transformed by the Spirit. It is what we call *lectio divina*. It consists of reading God's word in a moment of prayer and allowing it to enlighten and renew us. This prayerful reading of the Bible is not something separate from the study undertaken by the preacher to ascertain the central message of the text; on the contrary, it should begin with that study and then go on to discern how that same message speaks to his own life. The spiritual reading of a text must start with its literal sense. Otherwise we can easily make the text say what we think is convenient, useful for confirming us in our previous decisions, suited to our own patterns of thought.

Proclaiming the Gospel

The importance of deepening our understanding of God's salvation so that we can proclaim it more clearly and with more passion

Reflection on Scripture together
Romans 10.14–17

¹⁴But how are they to call on one in whom they have not believed? And how are they to believe in one of whom they have never heard? And how are they to hear without someone to proclaim him? ¹⁵And how are they to proclaim him unless they are sent? As it is written, 'How beautiful are the feet of those who bring good news!' ¹⁶But not all have obeyed the good news; for Isaiah says, 'Lord, who has believed our message?' ¹⁷So faith comes from what is heard, and what is heard comes through the word of Christ.

Explanatory note

In this part of Romans Paul is reflecting on why Israel has not taken advantage of the justification and salvation offered in the Gospel, though his reflections here give us an insight into what Paul believes to be the chain that leads to worship: someone is sent to proclaim, when they proclaim people can hear the Gospel, when they hear it they can believe it, when they believe it they can call on Christ.

The verb translated 'hear' might be better translated as 'listen to' as the key is not just hearing but hearing in such a way as makes a difference.

- Ask someone to read the passage through; keep a few moments' silence.

- Read the explanatory note above and spend a few minutes discussing any points that you notice.

- Then read the passage again (asking someone else to read it this time).

- Invite everyone to say a word or phrase which strikes them from the passage.

- Read the passage a third time; share together what this word or phrase means to you in your life and what questions it raises.

The proclamation of the gospel by the whole people of God
(based on 110–134)

Q

Being Church means being God's people ... This means that we are to be God's leaven in the midst of humanity. (114)

All the baptized, whatever their position in the Church or their level of instruction in the faith, are agents of evangelization, and it would be insufficient to envisage a plan of evangelization to be carried out by professionals while the rest of the faithful would simply be passive recipients. (120)

We should not think, however, that the Gospel message must always be communicated by fixed formulations learned by heart or by specific words which express an absolutely invariable content. (129)

The good news of God's love and salvation is for everyone, and all God's people are called to share it. No matter how long someone has been a Christian or how much they know, everyone who is baptized is called to share their faith. There can be no such thing as 'professional evangelizers' who do the task instead of everyone else. The Bible reminds us that Jesus sent people to proclaim him as soon as they had encountered him (like Andrew in John 1.41 or the Samaritan woman in John 4.39). Falling short of perfection is no excuse, we need to proclaim anyway while seeking to grow in the maturity of our faith. No one culture has a monopoly on faith in Jesus Christ, nor indeed is there only one way of proclaiming the gospel. All cultures and all people must find a way of proclaiming God's love that is genuine for them, whether it be through popular piety, conversation with others or other forms of culture.

Discuss

We tend to prefer to go on many training courses before we feel ready to share our faith with others. How do you feel about the model described here of going straight away to proclaim the good news like Andrew or the Samaritan woman did?

Pope Francis talks about the importance of popular piety within evangelization, in different places around the world this might include processions, statues etc. … In your context what might fall under the heading of popular piety and how might it be used in evangelism?

Imagine you were in the middle of a conversation with a friend. How might you weave in the proclamation of the good news of Jesus in a way that felt natural and not stilted?

Growing in maturity of faith
(based on 135–175)

It is worth remembering that 'the liturgical proclamation of the word of God, especially in the eucharistic assembly, is not so much a time for meditation and catechesis as a dialogue between God and his people, a dialogue in which the great deeds of salvation are proclaimed and the demands of the covenant are continually restated'. (137)

To speak from the heart means that our hearts must not just be on fire, but also enlightened by the fullness of revelation and by the path travelled by God's word in the heart of the Church and our faithful people throughout history. (144)

We are not asked to be flawless, but to keep growing and wanting to grow as we advance along the path of the gospel. (151)

Although we are sent to proclaim our faith immediately this does not mean that we should give up studying, learning and growing in our faith. One of the primary places where this can take place is in the homily at the Eucharist (the main Sunday service for Catholics). It is therefore very important for the preacher to think carefully about what they are doing when they preach. Preaching is not primarily about meditation or teaching but about encouraging a dialogue between God and his people; in order to achieve this preachers need not to have their hearts on fire but to know God's word in depth. This requires particular preparation, searching after truth and personalizing what is said to the congregation. Growth is not just about doctrinal formation but about leading people to an encounter with the Lord Jesus. Beauty is essential to this process but so is accompaniment, an accompaniment that teaches us to remove our sandals before the sacred ground of the other. Growth in Christian maturity must find its expression in the study of Scripture, and Scripture should be a door that is opened up to every believer.

Discuss

Pope Francis believes that the homily or sermon is one of the vital places where God enters into dialogue with his people. Has this been your experience? When you have heard God speak directly to you, how has this happened?

What do you think makes a really good homily or sermon?

What would you identify as some of the primary occasions where you have grown most in your Christian faith?

Closing worship

Light a candle – have a few moments of silence.

In the silence think about

● anything that has particularly challenged you in this session

● if there is anything you want to do differently from now on.

Spend a few minutes sharing your thoughts together, before either moving into a time of prayer or praying the final responses and prayers together.

How will people worship if they have never believed?
How beautiful are the feet of those who bring good news!

How will people believe if they have never listened?
How beautiful are the feet of those who bring good news!

How will people listen if no one proclaims?
How beautiful are the feet of those who bring good news!

How will people proclaim if no one sends them?
How beautiful are the feet of those who bring good news!

Amen

(taken from Isaiah 52.7; Romans 10.14–15)

As our Saviour taught us, so we pray: **Our Father**

And

**may the grace of our Lord Jesus Christ,
and the love of God,
and the fellowship of the Holy Spirit
be with us all
evermore.**

Amen.

The Social Dimension of Evangelization

Summary of Chapter 4, paragraphs 176–258

The heart of the gospel is life in community and engagement with others. If we receive God's love and love him in return then it follows that we will also desire, seek and protect the good of others. Many passages through the Bible remind us of the essential connection between salvation and love for our brothers and sisters. The gospel is not just about a personal relationship with God, it is about the kingdom of God. There are many ways in which our beliefs about the importance of the kingdom might find expression, but two great themes are especially important at this point in our history: the inclusion of the poor and the importance of peace.

The first theme – inclusion of the poor – lies at the heart of our faith: every individual Christian and every Christian community is called to work for the liberation of the poor so that they can be a full part of society. We are called to hear the cry of the poor and then to work to transform their lives and enhance their dignity. God's heart has a special place for the poor since they know the suffering of Christ. We need to allow ourselves to be evangelized by them. We also need to address the structural causes of poverty and to find ways to address inequality in our world. The second theme – peace – is equally important. Peace is not just the absence of violence nor does it justify unjust social structures. Peace involves a deep and lasting unity. Real peace requires us to deal well with conflict, not by ignoring it but by meeting it head-on and resolving it. Part of the role of evangelization is to pursue dialogue in many different forms as part of our search for peace.

Key extracts from Chapter 4

(Numbers at the start of each paragraph refer to the paragraph numbers in the document)

178. To believe in a Father who loves all men and women with an infinite love means realizing that 'he thereby confers upon them an infinite dignity'. To believe that the Son of God assumed our human flesh means that each human person has been taken up into the very heart of God. To believe that Jesus shed his blood for us removes any doubt about the boundless love which ennobles each human being. Our redemption has a social dimension because 'God, in Christ, redeems not only the individual person, but also the social relations existing between men'. To believe that the Holy Spirit is at work in everyone means realizing that he seeks to penetrate every human situation and all social bonds: 'The Holy Spirit can be said to possess an infinite creativity, proper to the divine mind, which knows how to loosen the knots of human affairs, even the most complex and inscrutable'. Evangelization is meant to co-operate with this liberating work of the Spirit.

187–8. Each individual Christian and every community is called to be an instrument of God for the liberation and promotion of the poor, and for enabling them to be fully a part of society … The word 'solidarity' is a little worn and at times poorly understood, but it refers to something more than a few sporadic acts of generosity. It presumes the creation of a new mind-set which thinks in terms of community and the priority of the life of all over the appropriation of goods by a few.

190. Sometimes it is a matter of hearing the cry of entire peoples, the poorest peoples of the earth, since 'peace is founded not only on respect for human rights, but also on respect for the rights of peoples'. Sadly, even human rights can be used as a justification for an inordinate defence of individual rights or the rights of the richer peoples. With due respect for the autonomy and culture of every nation, we must never forget that the planet belongs to all mankind and is meant for all mankind; the mere fact that some people are born in places with fewer resources or less development does not justify

the fact that they are living with less dignity. It must be reiterated that 'the more fortunate should renounce some of their rights so as to place their goods more generously at the service of others'.

192. Yet we desire even more than this; our dream soars higher. We are not simply talking about ensuring nourishment or a 'dignified sustenance' for all people, but also their 'general temporal welfare and prosperity'. This means education, access to health care, and above all employment, for it is through free, creative, participatory and mutually supportive labour that human beings express and enhance the dignity of their lives. A just wage enables them to have adequate access to all the other goods which are destined for our common use.

218. Peace in society cannot be understood as pacification or the mere absence of violence resulting from the domination of one part of society over others. Nor does true peace act as a pretext for justifying a social structure which silences or appeases the poor, so that the more affluent can placidly support their lifestyle while others have to make do as they can. Demands involving the distribution of wealth, concern for the poor and human rights cannot be suppressed under the guise of creating a consensus on paper or a transient peace for a contented minority. The dignity of the human person and the common good rank higher than the comfort of those who refuse to renounce their privileges. When these values are threatened, a prophetic voice must be raised.

5

Making the Kingdom Present in our World

— *The proclamation of the Gospel involves action as well as words, in particular listening to the cry of the poor and seeking peace*

Reflection on Scripture together

Luke 4.16–21

[16]When he came to Nazareth, where he had been brought up, he went to the synagogue on the Sabbath day, as was his custom. He stood up to read, [17]and the scroll of the prophet Isaiah was given to him. He unrolled the scroll and found the place where it was written: [18]'The Spirit of the Lord is upon me, because he has anointed me to bring good news to the poor. He has sent me to proclaim release to the captives and recovery of sight to the blind, to let the oppressed go free, [19]to proclaim the year of the Lord's favour.' [20]And he rolled up the scroll, gave it back to the attendant, and sat down. The eyes of all in the synagogue were fixed on him. [21]Then he began to say to them, 'Today this scripture has been fulfilled in your hearing.'

Explanatory note

When Jesus read from Isaiah 61.1–2 it is possible that it was the set reading of the day for the synagogue. In synagogues they heard first a piece of Scripture from the Torah and then a piece from the Prophets (known as the haftorah). This is still the custom in synagogues today.

It seems likely that the opening declaration: 'he has anointed me to bring good news to the poor' is then explained in what follows. Consequently proclaiming release, recovery of sight, etc. provides a more detailed explanation of what the good news is.

- Ask someone to read the passage through; keep a few moments' silence.

- Read the explanatory note above and spend a few minutes discussing any points that you notice.

- Then read the passage again (asking someone else to read it this time).

- Invite everyone to say a word or phrase which strikes them from the passage.

- Read the passage a third time; share together what this word or phrase means to you in your life and what questions it raises.

Care for the poor (based on 176–216)

Q

To evangelize is to make the kingdom of God present in our world. (176)

Our faith in Christ, who became poor, and was always close to the poor and the outcast, is the basis of our concern for the integral development of society's most neglected members. (186)

Small yet strong in the love of God, like Saint Francis of Assisi, all of us, as Christians, are called to watch over and protect the fragile world in which we live, and all its peoples. (216)

Evangelization is not just about words, it is about action too. The proclamation of the gospel has a very clear social content. It is not just about a personal relationship with God, it is also about caring for others. Right at the heart of our faith in Christ is a call to follow him in his care for the poor and the outcast. We are called to hear their cry and to stand in solidarity with them. Sometimes solidarity is misunderstood – it does not just mean occasional acts of generosity, but requires an entirely new outlook which thinks in terms of community, not just the appropriation of goods by a few. We are not just called to hear the voice of the poor, our dreams soar higher than this, we yearn to give them access to education, access to health care and employment.

Discuss

If you were to pick two themes that are fundamental to the way in which we live out the kingdom today. What would they be? Would they be the same two as Pope Francis' or different?

If we are to take seriously the call to hear the cry of the poor, to stand in solidarity with them and seek to transform their lives, what kind of things ought we, as individuals, to be doing? And what kind of things, as Christian communities, should we do?

What are you already doing for the poor? And what more might you think of doing?

The fruit of peace (based on 217–258)

Q

Peace in society cannot be understood as pacification or the mere absence of violence resulting from the domination of one part of society over others … 'it is fashioned by efforts directed day after day towards the establishment of the ordered universe willed by God, with a more perfect justice among men'. (218–219)

The message of peace is not about a negotiated settlement but rather the conviction that the unity brought by the Spirit can harmonize every diversity. (230)

By preaching Jesus Christ, who is himself peace (cf. Eph. 2.14), the new evangelization calls on every baptized person to be a peacemaker and a credible witness to a reconciled life. (239)

Another crucial social feature of evangelization involves seeking peace. There are four key principles which can guide people in this. Roughly speaking, these are that we need to be committed to setting up good processes which can bear fruit in the future, rather than to possessing all spaces of power in the present; that conflict cannot be ignored but needs to be faced and reconciled through the unity that comes from Christ; that there needs to be a dialogue between reality and ideas, you cannot dwell only in the realm of ideas; and that there is a tension between the global and the local but we need to broaden our horizons and always to keep the big picture in mind. Dialogue is also important as a contribution to peace. The Church needs to maintain a constant dialogue between faith, reason and science. It needs to support ecumenical dialogue, relations with Judaism and interreligious dialogue.

Discuss

How would you define peace? What needs to be present for peace to be genuine and not imposed?

Have you experienced an occasion when reconciliation has taken place (either in your life or the lives of other people). What were the factors that allowed or encouraged this to happen?

Why is dialogue important? What can it achieve?

Closing worship

Light a candle – have a few moments of silence.

In the silence think about

● anything that has particularly challenged you in this session

● if there is anything you want to do differently from now on.

Spend a few minutes sharing your thoughts together, before either moving into a time of prayer or praying the final responses and prayers together.

What does the Lord require of you?
God calls us to love justice

What does the Lord require of you?
God calls us to steadfast love

What does the Lord require of you?
**God calls us to walk humbly with him
Amen**

(taken from Micah 6.8)

As our Saviour taught us, so we pray: **Our Father**

And

**may the grace of our Lord Jesus Christ,
and the love of God,
and the fellowship of the Holy Spirit
be with us all
evermore.**

Amen.

Spirit-Filled Evangelizers

Summary of Chapter 5, paragraphs 259–288

The Holy Spirit gives us the courage to proclaim the gospel with boldness in every time and place, just as he did at Pentecost. We need to call on him through prayer because without prayer everything that we do will be fruitless and our message empty. Spirit-filled evangelizers are characterized by two things: prayer and work. Spiritual experiences without social and missionary outreach are of no help; outreach without prayer is vacuous and meaningless. The gospel responds to our deepest needs – friendship with Jesus and love of our brothers and sisters – and we need to find a way of expressing this so that others can encounter it too. We need to remind ourselves of our passion for what Jesus has done for us because without enthusiasm, certainty and love we can convince nobody. As well as being called into relationship with Jesus we are also called into deeper relationship with others. Mission involves a passion for Jesus as well as a passion for his people.

At the heart of what we believe lies the mysterious working of the risen Christ and of his Spirit. Christ's resurrection is not just a past event, it continues to permeate the world in which we live. Each day beauty is born anew. All who evangelize are agents of the power of resurrection. We can often not see the seeds of God's kingdom growing but the New Testament teaches us that no act of love for God will ever be lost. We may not see it but it will grow. One form of prayer that moves us to evangelization is intercessory prayer because it is focused on people. God's heart is touched by our intercession but we should be clear that he is always there first. Our intercession means that his power, love and faithfulness are shown more clearly in the midst of the people. With the Holy Spirit, Mary is always present in the midst of people, so we ask Mary to intercede that this invitation to a new phase of evangelization will be accepted by the whole Church, so that the Church may become a home for many peoples.

Key extracts from Chapter 5

(Numbers at the start of each paragraph refer to the paragraph numbers in the document)

261.   Whenever we say that something is 'spirited', it usually refers to some interior impulse which encourages, motivates, nourishes and gives meaning to our individual and communal activity. Spirit-filled evangelization is not the same as a set of tasks dutifully carried out despite one's own personal inclinations and wishes. How I long to find the right words to stir up enthusiasm for a new chapter of evangelization full of fervour, joy, generosity, courage, boundless love and attraction! Yet I realize that no words of encouragement will be enough unless the fire of the Holy Spirit burns in our hearts. A spirit-filled evangelization is one guided by the Holy Spirit, for he is the soul of the Church called to proclaim the gospel. Before offering some spiritual motivations and suggestions, I once more invoke the Holy Spirit. I implore him to come and renew the Church, to stir and impel her to go forth boldly to evangelize all peoples.

270.   Sometimes we are tempted to be that kind of Christian who keeps the Lord's wounds at arm's length. Yet Jesus wants us to touch human misery, to touch the suffering flesh of others. He hopes that we will stop looking for those personal or communal niches which shelter us from the maelstrom of human misfortune and instead enter into the reality of other people's lives and know the power of tenderness. Whenever we do so, our lives become wonderfully complicated and we experience intensely what it is to be a people, to be part of a people.

273.   My mission of being in the heart of the people is not just a part of my life or a badge I can take off; it is not an 'extra' or just another moment

in life. Instead, it is something I cannot uproot from my being without destroying my very self. I am a mission on this earth; that is the reason why I am here in this world. We have to regard ourselves as sealed, even branded, by this mission of bringing light, blessing, enlivening, raising up, healing and freeing. All around us we begin to see nurses with soul, teachers with soul, politicians with soul, people who have chosen deep down to be with others and for others. But once we separate our work from our private lives, everything turns grey and we will always be seeking recognition or asserting our needs. We stop being a people.

283. The great men and women of God were great intercessors. Intercession is like a 'leaven' in the heart of the Trinity. It is a way of penetrating the Father's heart and discovering new dimensions which can shed light on concrete situations and change them. We can say that God's heart is touched by our intercession, yet in reality he is always there first. What our intercession achieves is that his power, his love and his faithfulness are shown ever more clearly in the midst of the people.

288. There is a Marian 'style' to the Church's work of evangelization. Whenever we look to Mary, we come to believe once again in the revolutionary nature of love and tenderness. In her we see that humility and tenderness are not virtues of the weak but of the strong who need not treat others poorly in order to feel important themselves. Contemplating Mary, we realize that she who praised God for 'bringing down the mighty from their thrones' and 'sending the rich away empty' (Lk 1.52–53) is also the one who brings a homely warmth to our pursuit of justice. She is also the one who carefully keeps 'all these things, pondering them in her heart' (Lk 2.19). Mary is able to recognize the traces of God's Spirit in events great and small.

Being Filled by the Spirit

It is the Holy Spirit that gives us the courage to proclaim the gospel

Reflection on Scripture together

Luke 1.46–55

[46]*And Mary said,*

'My soul magnifies the Lord, [47]*and my spirit rejoices in God my Saviour,*
[48]*for he has looked with favour on the lowliness of his servant.*
Surely, from now on all generations will call me blessed;
[49]*for the Mighty One has done great things for me, and holy is his name.*
[50]*His mercy is for those who fear him from generation to generation.*
[51]*He has shown strength with his arm;*
he has scattered the proud in the thoughts of their hearts.
[52]*He has brought down the powerful from their thrones, and lifted up the lowly;*
[53]*he has filled the hungry with good things, and sent the rich away empty.*
[54]*He has helped his servant Israel, in remembrance of his mercy,*
[55]*according to the promise he made to our ancestors,*
to Abraham and to his descendants for ever.'

Explanatory note

The word translated 'magnify' corresponds to a Hebrew word used in the Old Testament (for example, Psalm 34.3; 69.30) to describe how a worshipper might relate to God. The implication is not that we can make God any greater than he already is. What we can do is to make God great in our lives in such a way as reflects his already existing greatness.

Many scholars identify this hymn with Hannah's song of praise in 1 Samuel 2.1–10. While it bears many similarities to that hymns Mary's song weaves in new themes of its own and suggests that it was not unusual to 'sing again' an Old Testament hymn in such a way as makes it new and relevant in the current context.

- Ask someone to read the passage through; keep a few moments' silence.

- Read the explanatory note above and spend a few minutes discussing any points that you notice.

- Then read the passage again (asking someone else to read it this time).

- Invite everyone to say a word or phrase which strikes them from the passage.

- Read the passage a third time; share together what this word or phrase means to you in your life and what questions it raises.

On being Spirit-filled evangelizers
(based on 259–274)

Q

Jesus wants evangelizers who proclaim the good news not only with words, but above all by a life transfigured by God's presence. (259)

How I long to find the right words to stir up enthusiasm for a new chapter of evangelization full of fervour, joy, generosity, courage, boundless love and attraction! Yet I realize that no words of encouragement will be enough unless the fire of the Holy Spirit burns in our hearts. (261)

> 'The missionary is convinced that, through the working of the Spirit, there already exists in individuals and peoples an expectation, even if an unconscious one, of knowing the truth about God, about man, and about how we are to be set free from sin and death.' (265)

The Spirit gives impetus for evangelization. Just as at Pentecost the Holy Spirit gave the disciples the necessary boldness to proclaim the good news of Jesus Christ, so also the Holy Spirit continues to do this today. Jesus does not want us to proclaim the good news in words alone but in lives that are transformed by God's presence. Spirit-filled evangelizers not only pray but also work. Prayer without work is no help at all; work without prayer leads to weariness and meaninglessness. It is the two together that brings transformation. The primary reason why we proclaim the good news is the love of Jesus. We need to beg him every day to open our hearts, and shake up our lukewarm and superficial existence. The enthusiasm of evangelizers comes from a conviction that everyone has an expectation of knowing the truth about God, about humanity, and about how we are to be set free from sin and death. Evangelization is about relationship: relationship with Jesus and relationship with others. It is not an additional extra that you can take off without destroying something about who you are.

Discuss

If we were to proclaim the good news with 'lives transfigured by God's presence', what kind of characteristics would you expect to find?

Do you agree that there is in everyone an expectation of knowing the truth about God?

Why is prayer so important for evangelization?

Prayer and Evangelism (based on 275–288)

> Some people do not commit themselves to mission because they think that nothing will change and that it is useless to make the effort. (275)
>
> Christ's resurrection is not an event of the past; it contains a vital power which has permeated this world. Where all seems to be dead, signs of the resurrection suddenly spring up. It is an irresistible force. (276)
>
> When evangelizers rise from prayer, their hearts are more open; freed of self-absorption, they are desirous of doing good and sharing their lives with others. (282)

Christ's resurrection has changed the world that we live in. Wherever there is darkness, fear and death, life breaks through stubbornly but invincibly. Christ's resurrection tells us that death is not the end, that life will always break through and that goodness always re-emerges and spreads. Belief in the resurrection keeps us going even when it looks as though there is no hope. Faith also entails believing in the love of God and that the kingdom will grow even when we can't see its growth. Intercessory prayer is vital for evangelization. Intercession becomes a prayer of gratitude to God as we begin to acknowledge what God is doing in the lives of others. This gratitude flows from a heart attentive to others but also brings us to a place of greater attention to those around us. God's heart is always touched by our intercession, though the reality is that he was always there in the first place.

Discuss

Can you think of an example of where you have seen evidence of Christ's resurrection in our world, where life has broken forth or goodness has re-emerged?

Why do you think that belief in the resurrection can keep us going when it feels as though there is no hope?

What do you think intercessory prayer achieves?

Closing worship

Light a candle – have a few moments of silence.

In the silence think about

● anything that has particularly challenged you in this session

● if there is anything you want to do differently from now on.

Spend a few minutes sharing your thoughts together, before either moving into a time of prayer or praying the final responses and prayers together.

When we lack boldness in your gospel
Fill us with your Spirit, O Lord

When we lose faith in your love
Fill us with your Spirit, O Lord

When our passion flags
Fill us with your Spirit, O Lord

Then send us out, in the power of that Spirit,
to proclaim your love, justice and peace

Amen

(taken from Micah 6.8)

As our Saviour taught us, so we pray: **Our Father**

And

**may the grace of our Lord Jesus Christ,
and the love of God,
and the fellowship of the Holy Spirit
be with us all
evermore.**

Amen.

Glossary

As you read through the document, you may come across some words that are unfamiliar, especially if you are not Catholic; this brief glossary maybe helpful.

Acedia
: a word particularly associated with those in religious orders and identified as a state of torpor or listlessness so great that you cannot even pray.

Catechesis
: religious instruction of any kind.

Evangelization
: the word more often used in a Catholic context and often means the same as evangelism. Where it differs in emphasis would be that evangelism often means specific acts of witness, whereas evangelization is a broader word used to describe the entire calling and nature of the Church, and overlaps in meaning with the word 'mission'.

Kerygma
: the good news that we preach.

Mystagogy
: the ongoing instruction of a Christian through his or her life and faith-journey.

Parrhesia
: the Greek word for boldness.

Sensus Fidei
: literally the sense of faith – it is a consensus of belief that comes from the whole people of God and gives witness to the truth of a doctrine.